## Second Edition

# D'Nealian®

# Handwriting

**Author**

*Donald Neal Thurber*

## Independent Practice Book/2

### FOR BOOK TWO

## Scott, Foresman and Company

Editorial Offices: Glenview, Illinois
Regional Offices: Sunnyvale, California • Tucker, Georgia •
Glenview, Illinois • Oakland, New Jersey • Dallas, Texas

ISBN 0-673-27342-3
1991 Impression
Copyright © 1987
Scott, Foresman and Company, Glenview, Illinois
All Rights Reserved
Printed in the United States of America

D'Nealian is a registered trademark of Donald Neal Thurber.



1920212223-WEB-009998979695

# Contents

# D'Nealian Philosophy of Handwriting

The D'Nealian™ Handwriting Program was developed in the late 1960s by an experienced teacher, Donald Neal Thurber. The model letters of this manuscript alphabet are somewhat different from other alphabets. The letters slant, and ending strokes make it easy for children to convert to cursive handwriting.

The D'Nealian philosophy includes respect for individuality as long as size, form, slant, and spacing are consistent. Handwriting that is readable is acceptable. The program introduces letters in groups that are formed by similar writing strokes. Relying only on letters previously learned, children immediately write words that are presented in a meaningful context.

Name

Practice

ā                                                    a

a

A                                                    A

A

Alabama and Alaska

Practice Some More

a                    A

Ada wasn't afraid.

Name

Practice

d     d

d

D     D

D

Did Don dry dishes?

Practice Some More

d     D

Dogs do get muddy.

Name

Practice

o    o

o

O    O

O

on to Oregon

Practice Some More

o    O

Open both doors.

Name

Practice

g          g

g

G          G

G

Greg grows grapes.

Practice Some More

g          G

Gil and Gigi agree.

Name

Practice

c          c

c

C          C

C

Cecile | Carla | Chuck

Practice Some More

c          C

Cora checks chicks.

D'Nealian™ Handwriting    Scott, Foresman
Name
Practice
e
e
E
E
Ellen met Evelyn.
Practice Some More
e    E
Eddie sees Eve.

Name

Practice

s    S

s

S    S

S

Sis saw Suki's suit.

Practice Some More

s    S

Susie served soup.

**Name**

**Practice**

f    f

f

F    F

F

Fran | Floyd | Flora

**Practice Some More**

f    F

Fred Fluff found it.

Name

Practice

*b*             *b*

*b*

*B*             *B*

*B*

*Bill Bell buys books.*

Practice Some More

*b*             *B*

*Bob broke both bats.*



Writing Manuscript **bB**   9

**Name**

**Practice**

l                                                                    l

l

L                                                                   L

L

Larry | Lillian | Lloyd

**Practice Some More**

l                              L

Lolly looks like Lil.

D'Nealian™ Handwriting    Scott, Foresman

Name

Practice

t                                    t
t
T                                    T
T

Tom took Toto too.

Practice Some More

t            T

That turtle is Ted's.

D'Nealian Handwriting™, Second Edition, Book 2, © Scott, Foresman and Company.
This page may not be reproduced without written permission.

Writing Manuscript tT    11

Name

Practice

h       h

h

H       H

H

Hilary | Hugh | Henry

Practice Some More

h       H

Hold your head high.

Name

Practice

k          k

k

K          K

K

Kimiko | Kurt | Kenji

Practice Some More

k          K

Karl kept on skating.

Name

Practice

*i*        *i*

*i*

*I*        *I*

*I*

*Iris is Ida's sister.*

Practice Some More

*i*        *I*

*Is Ivan Ides inside?*

Name

Practice

u                    u

u

U                    U

U

Ula unrolled a rug.

Practice Some More

u          U

Use our tuba, Uri.

Name

Practice

w                                                w

w

W                                                W

W

Where was Wally?

Practice Some More

w                    W

Which wolf is wild?

Name

Practice

y          y

y

Y          Y

Y

Yoko, it's your yoyo.

Practice Some More

y          Y

You may stay today.

Name

Practice

j

j

j

J

J

Jump into Jo's jeep.

Practice Some More

j        J

Jan joined in July.

Name

Practice

r          r

r

R          R

R

Red Robin chirped.

Practice Some More

r          R

Rich ran in the rain.

Name

Practice

*n*                                                    *n*

*n*

N                                                    N

N

*Norma* | *Nancy* | *Ned*

Practice Some More

*n*                            N

*Nelson knows Neil.*

Name

Practice

m          m

m

M          M

M

Mae made muffins.

Practice Some More

m          M

Mom makes maps.

Name

Practice

p        p

p

P        P

P

Paul | Philip | Polly

Practice Some More

p     P

Please pay Pepe.

Name

Practice

q          q

q

Q          Q

Q

Quincy is quiet.

Practice Some More

q          Q

Quenby quit quickly.

Name

Practice

Vicky | Vivian | Velma

Practice Some More

Vance visited Vera.

Name

Practice

Z    z

z

Z    Z

Z

Zebras dozed lazily.

Practice Some More

z    Z

Zoe raises zinnias.

Name

Practice

x

x

x

*Xio expects a box.*

Practice Some More

x          X

*X rays start at six.*

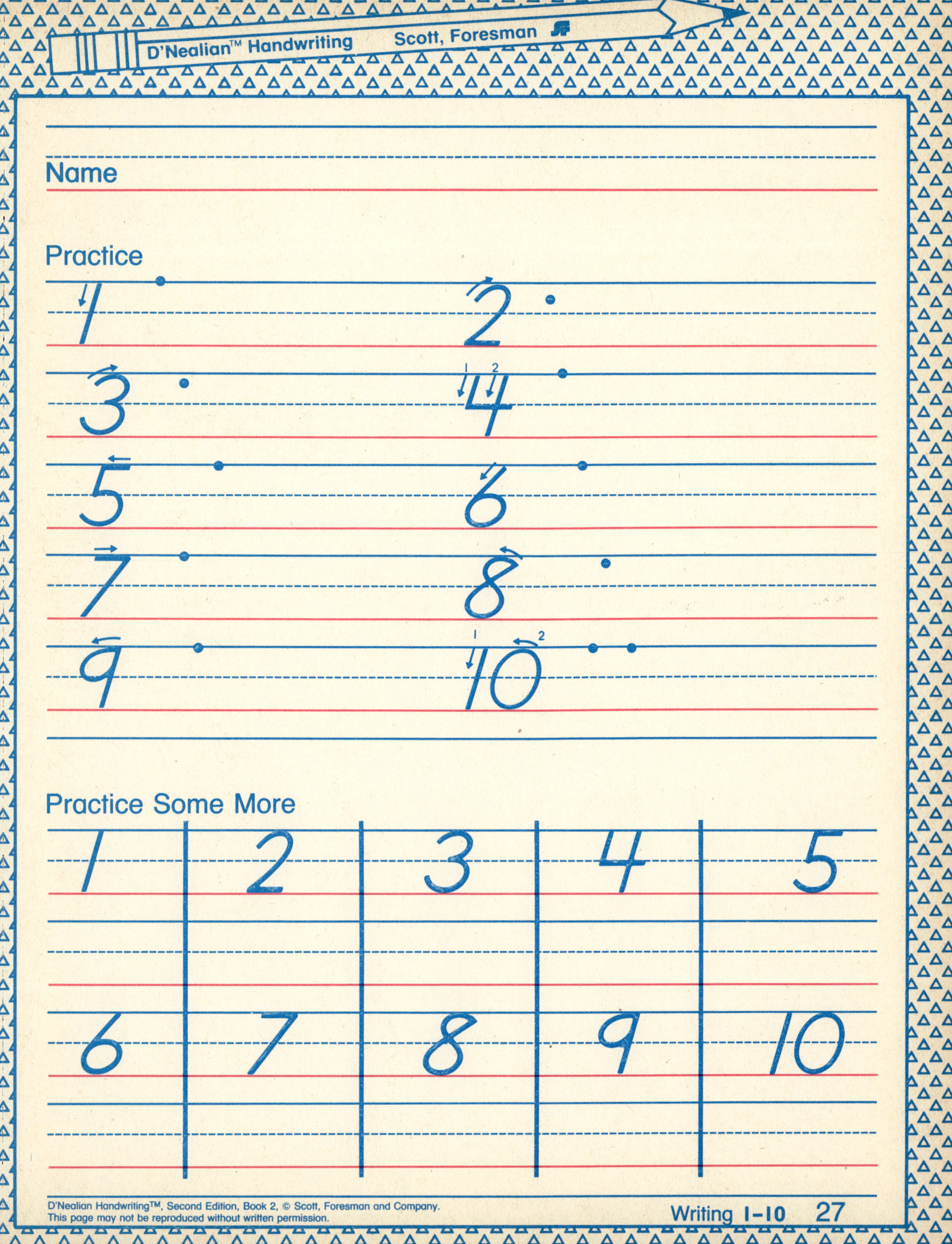

D'Nealian™ Handwriting     Scott, Foresman
Name
Practice
1
2
3
4
5
6
7
8
9
10
Practice Some More
1  2  3  4  5
6  7  8  9  10

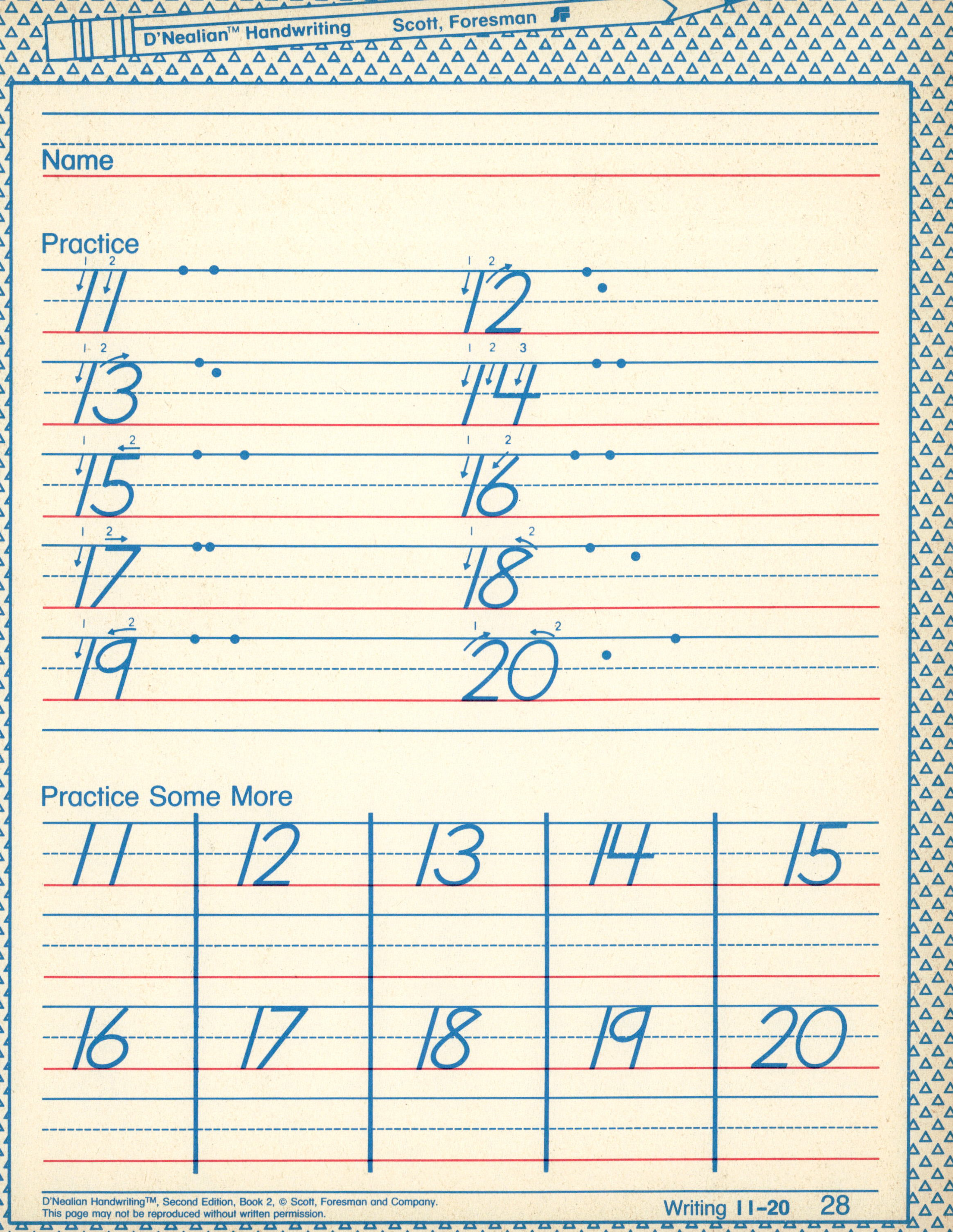


**Name**

**Practice**



**Practice Some More**

Name

Practice

*l*

*l*

*l*

*l*

Practice Some More

*ll*

*ll*

*ll*

*ll*

Name

Practice

*h* .                          *h*

*h*

*h*

*h*

Practice Some More

*hh*

*lh*

*hl*

*hlh*

Name

Practice

_k_ .

_k_

_k_

_k_

Practice Some More

_kk_

_lk_

_hk_

_kh_

Name

Practice

Practice Some More

**Name**

**Practice**

i                                                                              i

i

i

i

**Practice Some More**

ti

il

it | hi | till

Name

Practice

Practice Some More



Writing Cursive **u**     34

**Name**

**Practice**

*e .*        *e*

*e*

*tell* | *he* | *heel*

**Practice Some More**

*ee*

*the kite*

*little elk teeth*

**Name**

**Practice**

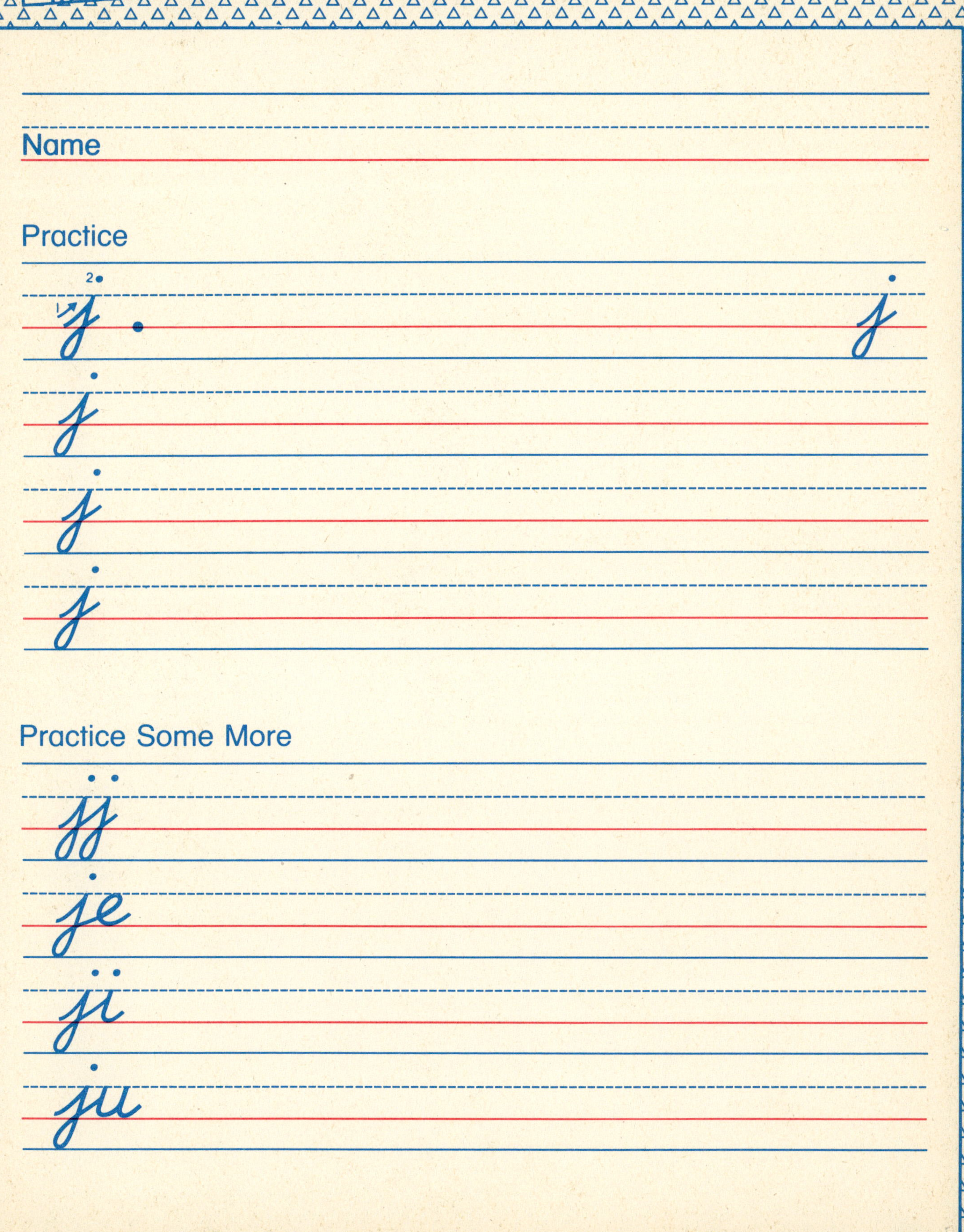

**Practice Some More**

Name

Practice

p .                                          p

p

pull | up | help

Practice Some More

pu

the pet pup

the jeep he'll keep

Name

Practice

a .                                                    a

a

hall | at | apple

Practice Some More

al

all that talk

at a lake

Name

Practice

d .        d

d

lid | did | added

Practice Some More

dd

a dull thud

a deep, deep puddle

Name

Practice

c .                                                        c

c

cut | cat | pick

Practice Some More

ch

a latch catch

tick, tick, click

**Name**

**Practice**

n.        n

n

needle and pin

**Practice Some More**

nn

pen and pencil

neat, clean kennel

Name

Practice

m .                     m

m

me | am | hummed

Practice Some More

mp

camp mail time

lame tame camel



Writing Cursive **m**     42

Name

Practice

Practice Some More

Name

Practice

*g* .                                                              *g*

*g*

*get* | *egg* | *tagging*

Practice Some More

*gg*

*laughing again*

*a huge digging pig*

Name

Practice

y .                                                          y

y

yell | may | they

Practice Some More

my

any play clay

my tiny puppy

**Name**

**Practice**

q   q

q

q

q

**Practice Some More**

qu

eq

queen | quit | equal

Name

Practice

*o*                                                    *o*

*o*

| *noon* | *too* | *good* |

Practice Some More

*oo*

*going to the moon*

*one cool pool*

Name

Practice

w            w

w

| who | how | two |

Practice Some More

wi

new wide window

white down pillow

Name

Practice

*b*                  *b*

*b*

| *been* | *about* | *gobble* |

Practice Some More

*bb*

*a blue baby bib*

*a big bobbing bubble*

Name

Practice

*v*    *v*

*v*

velvet glove

Practice Some More

ve

lovely evening view

a paved avenue

Name

Practice

z                  z

z

| zone | puzzle | dizzy |

Practice Some More

zz

a dizzy zooming bee

hazy, lazy day

Name

Practice

s .             s

s

| sits | glass | season |

Practice Some More

ss

last school classes

six slick slides

Name

Practice

r .                                                                    r

r

very merry parrot

Practice Some More

rr

large roaring tiger

rare berry tree

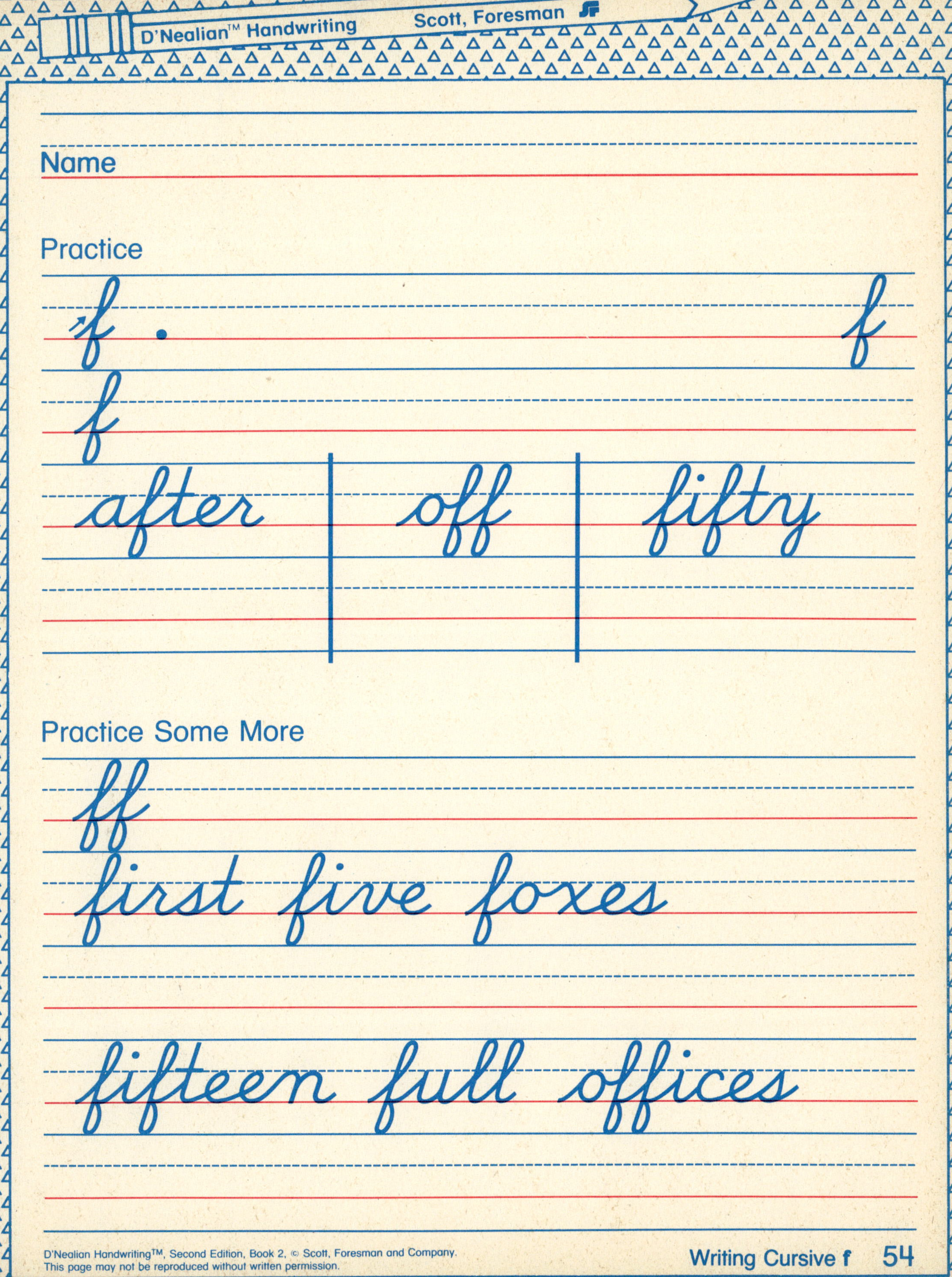

Name

Practice
f
f
after | off | fifty

Practice Some More
ff
first five foxes
fifteen full offices

Name

Practice

Á    *a*

*a*

*Alex* | *Ana* | *Adam*

Practice Some More

*A*

*Al and Amy argued.*

*Ask about Anita.*

Name

Practice

*C*                                                                                          *C*

*C*

Come to Colorado.

Practice Some More

*C*

Cat called Cecile.

Candy Cat is cuddly.

Name

Practice

$\mathcal{E}$

$\mathcal{E}$          $\mathcal{E}$

Eli | Ethel | Elmer

Practice Some More

$\mathcal{E}$

Edi Ellis ate early.

Eva enjoyed Egypt.

Name

Practice

*O*                                    *O*

*O*

*Orson*        *Olivia*        *Oz*

Practice Some More

*O*

*Olga drove to Ohio.*

*Oscar spoke to Otto.*

Name

Practice

H        H

H

Hugo | Holly | Horace

Practice Some More

H

Harley heard Hugh.

How did Hazel help?

Name

Practice

K         K

K

Kansas | Kentucky

Practice Some More

K

Ken lives in Keokuk.

King Kurt is kind.

Name

Practice

*n*                                                                                          *n*

*n*

*Nellie of Nevada*

Practice Some More

*n*

*Nurse Nora is nice.*

*Nan is Nick's niece.*

**Name**

**Practice**

m                 m

m

Mario missed Mac.

**Practice Some More**

m

Moe met Mr. Mills.

Myra came in May.

Name

Practice

*U*

*U*

Uri | Una | Ursa

Practice Some More

*U*

Up went Ugo's kite.

Uncle Uri laughed.

Name

Practice

V ·                                                    V

V

| Vince | Van | Victor |

Practice Some More

V

Visit Vermont.

Valerie saved Vicky.

Name

Practice

W W

W

Why did Walt wait?

Practice Some More

W

Was Wes working?

Wally watched Will.

Name

Practice

*Y*

*Y*

*Y*

Yonkers, New York

Practice Some More

*Y*

Yes, it is Yolanda.

Yancy is in Yuma.

Name

Practice

$T$ · $T$

$T$

Tim | Tina | Theresa

Practice Some More

$T$

Todd told Terry.

There goes Tomas.

**Name**

**Practice**

F       F

F

Ford's Fun Fair

**Practice Some More**

F

Freda Franks fell.

Fritz fixed Flo's fife.

Name

Practice

B             B

B

Babs is beautiful.

Practice Some More

B

Bob's balloon burst.

Bring Bernie's book.

Name

Practice

P                                   P

P

Please help Pat.

Practice Some More

P

Pablo pleased Pete.

Paul paints in Paris.

Name

## Practice

R

R

R

Rachel | Rita | Rory

## Practice Some More

R

Red River ran dry.

Rand Road is rough.

Name

## Practice

*G* .        *G*

*G*

| Gus | Gene | Gerry |

## Practice Some More

*G*

Gene greeted Glen.

Gayle is in Georgia.

Name

Practice

S.　　　　　S

S

Sally | Sonny | Stan

Practice Some More

S

She spoke to Sam.

Sid stood by Sue.

Name

Practice

l                                                    l

l

Irene in Iceland

Practice Some More

l

Ira visited Iowa.

Is it Igor Ives?

Name

Practice

$Q$ .                $Q$

$Q$

Quentin | Quimby

Practice Some More

$Q$

Quick, quit quacking.

Queenie was quiet.

Name

Practice

Zena isn't lazy.

Practice Some More

Zoe Zell felt dizzy.

Zip up Zeb's coat.

Name

Practice

*D*                                    *D*

*D*

*Did Dan know?*

Practice Some More

*D*

*Dale is my dad.*

*Did Dr. Dee drive?*

Name

Practice

$\mathcal{J}$ .    $\mathcal{J}$

$\mathcal{J}$

January and June

Practice Some More

$\mathcal{J}$

Jay Jones told Jill.

Joe is just joking.

Name

## Practice

$\chi$  ·  $\chi$

$\chi$

$\chi$

$\chi$

## Practice Some More

$\chi a$

$\chi e$

$\chi$ marks the spot.

Name

Practice

*L*           *L*

*L*

*Leave Lucy alone.*

Practice Some More

*L*

*Lady Lily is lovely.*

*Lena Linn listened.*

a b c d e f g h i j k l m
n o p q r s t u v w x y z
A B C D E F G
H I J K L M N O P Q
R S T U V W X Y Z
a b c d e f g h i j k
l m n o p q r s t
u v w x y z    , . ?
A B C D E F G H I
J K L M N O P Q R
S T U V W X Y Z
1 2 3 4 5 6 7 8 9 10